Streets After Rain

Streets after Rain

Poems by
Elizabeth Knies

Library of Congress Catalogue Card Number 80-66181
ISBN 0-914086-31-6

Printed in the United States of America

Cover watercolor by Susan Bienen Johnson
Book design by George Lallas
Photo by Sandy Agrafiotis

Typeset by Leora Zeitlin & Ed Hogan
Aspect Composition
13 Robinson St., Somerville, Mass. 02145

Also by Elizabeth Knies: *The New Year & Other Poems,*
published in *Threesome Poems,* Alice James Books, 1976.

Special thanks to the editors of the following
publications, where some of these poems, or
versions thereof, have appeared: *The Newbury-
port Current, Green House, The Hudson Review,
Penumbra, Scratchgravel Hills*

The publication of this book was assisted by a grant
from the Massachusetts Council on the Arts & Humanities

Alice James Books are published by the Alice James
Poetry Cooperative, Inc.

Alice James Books
138 Mt. Auburn Street
Cambridge, Massachusetts 02138

for my friends

Contents

Erinnerung

Und du wartest, erwartest das Eine
das dein Leben unendlich vermehrt;
das Mächtige, Ungemeine,
das Erwachen der Steine,
Tiefen, dir zugekehrt.

Es dämmern im Bücherständer
die Bände in Gold und Braun;
und du denkst an durchfahrene Länder,
an Bilder, an die Gewänder
wiederverlorener Fraun.

Und da weisst du auf einmal: Das war es.
Du erhebst dich, und vor dir steht
eines vergangenen Jahres
Angst und Gestalt und Gebet.

—*Rainer Maria Rilke*
Das Buch Der Bilder

Remembering

And you wait, are waiting for the One
that will endlessly enlarge your life;
the vast, the extraordinary,
the awakening of stones,
depths that turn toward you.

Dawning in the bookcase
bindings in gold and brown;
and you think of countries passed through,
of pictures, of the gowns
of women lost over and over.

And suddenly you know: That was it.
You arise, and before you there
stands a past year's anguish
and form and prayer.

11

I.
Things
of Absolute
Necessity

*The trees are queued in an endless line
in the fading light.
They wait, snow-bound, arms raised.*

And it is a year, another, a new year.

Rooms

1.

A house above a river, the water
coursing by, green
in the morning,
evenings blue,
the hours pass
I tend my plants
and think about the nature of things

The angle of my looking
brings the water close to the door,
flanked by cedar and spruce
stone steps lead up
strewn with pine needles

Close to earth
crocuses and the *iris reticulata* have bloomed...

even in darkness they are there

2.

I stay up late,
reading and poking the fire...

This is the solitude I dreamed,
the singular settling down, the peace
of rooms where no one moves...

Here, the sand will not run through.
Time dissolves, unnecessary.

Here I can garner my strength,
become a still center.

Here I can do no wrong.

3.

Dark night.
One, two, three of the clock.
Shapes on the ceiling flicker,
merge, separate into profiles,
a man and a woman
facing each other   looking, looking.

My eyes are dry, painfully dry.
My heart continues to beat.

4.

(things of absolute necessity)

To water the ivy
so that its tendrils
can continue to inch
toward the light.
To look out the window
on the cold, clean
measures of snow,
printed with birds,
strewn with husks of seeds.
To hold, keep holding.

5.

grey on grey
riverwater and sky
flowing

a house
suspended
in fog

the rain comes
heavily
the window runs

with tears
blurry images
a tree

leafing
cars on a bridge
lightning

6.

walls
grey-blue
the feather of a pigeon
music
someone else is playing
muted and mingled
sounds
the world
goes about its business
below my windows
below the sky

7.

At last I got what I bargained for,
the chance to sleep and wake
far from your care.

(a sleepwalker stalking the rooms
    upstairs, downstairs, up again)

They are just what I wanted   spare
and clean, without connotations, without past,
without perplexity. I will sleep
in them the deep sleep of solitude,
of death-in-life beneath the figured ceilings.

Against Ruin

Your books and papers piled on your table
in a small house where you are struggling to keep warm
this winter; my books and papers
piled on my desk. Emblems
chaotic, various. What will emerge
will not be a grand plan, nothing to save the universe,
but fragments shored against ruin, the warmth
of a stove against the enormous cold.

Out there the beach is a wide deserted arc
windswept and hard,
the sand rippled from the water pulling back.
This is what we know.
Let us walk, then, together along the shore,
our breath forming one breath in the cold air.
Let us walk and talk together like the friends we are.

Signs

I.

I used to ask
for a sign;
it was a form
of praying

I would look up
at the sky
across the expanse
of sea, waiting

I thought
I should see
a silver mourning dove
plummet from heaven

or flames
leap in tongues
on the caps of the waves.

None of these things
happened;
there was only
the sky's variable blue
the flat
indifferent sea

II.

The dark
leaves a black sound
out there, in air

a year
goes by
it is summer

wires
carry our voices
across the night

"I worry about you."

emotion's
margin, the fraction
of care

delicately
removed
from the eye

the geranium
blown over by wind
has a broken stem

still green,
it hangs
by a thin fiber

Two Poems

Dear one,
          will I never again
feel your breath on my cheek, in sleep?
Gall, bitterness are mine,
I am lost in the deeps
with nothing to guide by, neither compass nor stars.
And on the horizon
the black ship gliding calmly and true,
the black ship where a berth is already saved for me.

*

Illumined by your clear
unflinching eye, our dread time.
Penelope, Antigone, Leukothea
linger here
vivid in your retelling,
taking on flesh, retrieved.

Look again into legend and see
a woman who had once been forgiven
weeping beside a tomb; the great stone door
open, and the gardener yet to appear.

A voice across some far place calling
some canyon chasm   dry   parched
and I, trying to reach—

feet heavy, sinking in clay
or again in ash, light powdery ash
that rises in clouds to choke,
conceal. Downdrift of all...
faint voice, faint call.

Allow the Light

What would be full of light
must first be dark, may be;
as morning lights the sky slowly
and sight returns, substantial forms
resume their surety. Count on this,
the other darkness need not overwhelm.
             Allow the light
to ease your mind, spirit, heart.
Let it. It will not fail.

New Castle, New Hampshire

I go out and sit in the sun
at the small beach cupped like a palm
to receive the bright coin of the sea.
The sea here has no waves; its rhythm,
almost inaudible, pulses
in the flux of black seaweed and kelp.
If you sit on the farthest outcropping of rocks
the water will gradually seep around you
until you are adrift, and must cross
an icy moat to return to shore.
There are no shells to speak of, no souvenirs
except smooth obloid stones
and the prolific minutiae of the tidepools.
Mothers and children and babysitters contend.
Young men and women offer up
their bodies to the sun.
The wind blows sand onto their sticky skin
and onto the pages of the book
I am trying to read. I put it down,
and search the blue haze of the Atlantic
for the memory of my first sight of the Mediterranean.
Years ago, when we topped a hill in southern France
on our bikes, it lay below us, as blue as they said.

This summer
you are in the Outer Hebrides to see the Celtic landscape
before it falls to the avarice of the oil companies,
and I am coming to terms with my own life,
solitary and slow, for once without haste.
Things settle
and the whole of the past assumes its rightful place.
It may be that the coming-together and the going-apart
are really one motion.
I watch the children dally along the shore,
the cheerful progress of colored sails;
farther off, the floating image of the Isles of Shoals.

Circles

The light at this hour
benign, clear.
Swirls in the carpet—
motes in the air
of childhood.

The round table you made
and brought home in sunlight that day
now here in this room.

Years of light
between us, light years.
I reach out my hand
to that hollow
place. I feel it
as one explores
an old wound, the flesh
bunched and scarred.

The light describes circles
along the wall. I see
things differently now:
each day
transforms
into another day.

II.

Into
the Frame

What more can we ask of the beautiful than this,
that it be there to look upon,
passing before our astonished eyes
with salutations and farewells unlike our own.

Two Scenes

Long in coming, this
has changed the gist of what it was
to be suspended in a clock
without hours or meaning.

Now I have regained the world
things press upon me in a crowd,
I am the blind who speak
in miracles of sight.

And the scales fall—
they continue to fall—
I walk in a perpetual
first knowledge.

Wet and green
the grass dazzles, the trees
put out their leaves
perfect in every part.

*

What transpires
does not defy description—
it has been painted often.
So I have often thought

when swimming in a pond
rimmed with trees
of Cezanne's dark green,
angular pines

mirrored in water
near the bridge at Maincy.
Reflected,
they form a double presence in the world.

And I, floating upon stillness,
mingle with two elements:
a net of dark branches
above and beneath.

Freedom

I wake to bells on a Sunday morning
and float in the big bed
                        largesse
it is almost like being loved, to lie here
in such peace. And I will be inspired
by thoughts of the world beyond the wide windowsills
lined with geraniums. I chose this.

You, on a wooden deck in the arms of trees,
surrounded by potted plants with their trailing vines,
look up almost directly at the sun.
You will its shining. It swells with pride
that you turn like a leaf to its light.

Full Moon

Striated leaves, white and green,
hang in the moonlight. Although
the air is absolutely still
they seem to quiver,
pale and luminous
in the moonlight slanting
through the pane.
All this is of another world.

Streets After Rain

After three days of rain
I walk, at evening, the green streets.
The clouds turn salmon, then pink,
then the light leaves them.
A thin moon glides.
In the houses lights come on.

Under the black, wet maples
I think of the contours of your body,
its suppleness and grace,
your skin glistening like the streets after rain.

The Women

The women in bright-colored dresses
come toward you in a steady stream.
You take them into your arms like roses,
crushed carmine, a beautiful bouquet.

I sit on the sidelines with my wine
pale in the glass, chill as my blood,
and follow this curious event
in this room hot with sex and jazz.

My sisters, I wonder at my penchant for pain—
I draw it like a lot out of a jar.
Unerringly my hand, from among the thousand choices,
selects the fateful number.

Midsummer

Now I must unwind
what had been carefully wound.
The light is blinding. The heat stifling.
Disasters occur with some frequency in such weather.
Crops and power fail.
I look for comfort   the pages of books
but in fact I don't know where to turn.
Let's go away somewhere
high in the mountains.
For us, the mountain lake would part
like silk sheets.
We would watch the water darken and the stars come out.
Mine would be the illusion of permanence and peace,
yours, of perfect freedom.

The Party

Against the pale sky
of evening
the music
flies up,
a flock
of tropical birds.

I am looking down
on the heads
of all these people
looking into
each other's eyes.

They assume
graceful poses,
whisper
intimate things.

To me, the young men say,
"You are out of the 19th
century."

Down the sloping lawn
I look
at you, a dark figure
in a constellation
of music.

Love and pain
tangle in my heart.

Already this scene
is speeding away,
blazing like a meteor shower
in the August night.

Those Mornings

The world fits into itself. Its arms
hold all that breathes. The window
keeps sadness out and us within.
Gaunt pines circle in the slight wind.
I am folded in your arms.

*

Those mornings
are committed to memory. The frieze
of pines, sun on the bark. To the present,
and to the unimaginable future
they already lend their warmth.

Eire

for Larry Millman

From you I have these solitary images
of storytellers stranded on islands off the west,
subsisting, making do, with peat fires and spuds.

This desirable life
you found on the bare islands, and could not explain.
Life is richer there, you said.

Standing up in the sea
the rough islands cast their inhabitants from them
because they could not eke out a life.

A livelihood. Inishbofin and Inisheer and Clare
slowly deserted until what is left
is very nearly what it began with, before it was named.

You did not make it a metaphor
for all the world, but I saw it
and marveled, and was somehow consoled

to think of men in curraghs who paddle for fish,
their faces like jewels in the prongs of the sea.
Fishermen, singers, tellers of tales.

Rehearsals

for Marie

Before the words are out the meaning reverses,
and yet we try to pin it down.

We who are good at words
cannot find our voices.

(this stiff knot-at-the-heart that will not loosen,
      this pain, with and without tears)

Come then.   Be calm.   It will be summer
in a meadow   white, green and gold,

the sibilant insects and wind through high grass,
the voices of your children

and a clear sky cool upon your forehead, tender.
Everything you need will be there.

An Afternoon in Late November

Looking at the paintings of Louisa Mattiasdottir,
daughter of Iceland, who paints with a bold, blunt hand,
geometrics of little colored houses
and clean street scenes, as if much
of modern life had not touched there.
The sky, clouds, and protruding hills
plied into good forms,
the people, large in the landscape, but anonymous.
A still life that takes the eye—
lemons and limes in a dish,
the paint "buttery."
Best of all, two outsized Iceland sheep,
one white, one black, stand firm
and gaze out from the neutral plane
with pure presence.

Rain

Rain handles the house,
smoothes the contours
like a child working clay.

The shape keeps changing—
now squat, now tall
little rows of windows, chimneys, a door...

I strain, nearsighted, to the glass.
Wavering clumps of trees, sprawled gardens.
It may all wash away.

....*etwas fehlt.* What is it?
I thumb through pages anxiously
looking for a single word.

This Weather

1.

The hurricane warnings are up—
along the coast, the tourists scatter—
lobstermen to traps
set in the roiling sea—
householders to batten
glass and frame against the furious wind.
The wind, the rain
have been with us now for days.
We wait. We follow the storm's progress
and the tide's crest.
It is the full moon, too.

2.
This weather.
Full leaf
black in the shadows.
A puzzle? A movie?

Above
is fretwork, counterpoint.
Various harmonies.

Sotto voce
Molto espressionato

Clear

3.

Late night and first snow
under the streetlights,
fog horn muffled from far away.
Creature comforts of clanking pipes,
water running in the next apartment,
my upstairs neighbor gently rummaging about,
careful not to disturb me.

Such things might gladden the heart
on a cold night, in winter,
in a distant country.

4.

All I can see is the watery sky—
white rinsed with blue—
a bird's nest
suspended in the earth's caught breath.
How frail everything is,
traced with snow.
The only movement is a dark shape
flying into and out of the frame.

5.

Narrow
room and
heart in slack time,
in-drawn: alive still, barely.
Under snow
a motion: the stream's
vein needling through rock bed.
Ice over cress
sharp green.

Darkness: Light

Impossible
to know how it happened
the leaves
are full-bodied
again
darkly glossed
by late spring rain
their wet faces
turned to the wind
and they shine
in the darkness
they shine

How instructive
are the leaves
in streetlight—
watching them
I think I understand
this curious sensation
that rises like sap
and lodges near the heart

Song

The rose unfolds
from the cold closed bud—
whorl upon whorl
of lucent red—
attar of roses
all things under the sun
have their place and plan
in presence and in absence loved

Kesa

gliding on little feet
through your paper house
wrapped in embroidered robes
petals of a rose

you kneel to the koto
tilting your head
black hair flowing   a black river

*

the window is open
to the street sounds of summer
lilacs in great clusters
bloom all over town
half a year
is like the opening of a hand

I Look Out

and the world is closed tight.
Buckled and numb, I can't speak.
Stars float in an iron kettle
above the moon's struck match.

Where are the colors?
Black is the presence of all
but all falls back
into the shadow-world.

Remember, there is still the garden
under the lights,
lit fountains   hundreds of flowers,
nicotiana releasing the essence
of late summer.

There, when you can't sleep
on sultry nights, nothing moves:
not even the tall, frail cosmos
twined in forgetfulness,
not even the lights on the black water.

Legend

We go everywhere. Slats of sunlight
through the trees,
our faces flickering.

This is a procession. Cloth-of-gold,
carnelian, emerald.
We ride slowly, with dignity.
The green
of the forest surrounds.

You have appeared once again.
My body bears the marks of your love.
My skin smells of you, the scent
of *fraises des bois.*

Chrysanthemums

for Dale

The tea tray is set by the bed.
You read to me
Rexroth's translations of Tu Fu.
Among the pillows
and the slate blue walls,
the shine of your living hair,
your quiet voice.
The short poems
of pain, sadness, separation,
aging and death
carry across hundreds of years
to reassure us
as we lie here
with the late morning sun
warming the room,
'lost between heaven and earth.'